Open Immigration: Yea

A FREER IMMIGRATION policy is a necessary component of a free-market economic system, and it is an important attribute of a society that values the principles of individual liberty and constitutionally limited government. Restrictive immigration policies are government tools of social, demographic, and economic engineering that are unacceptably intrusive and contrary to those principles of liberty.

Many American conservatives who generally support those important principles are also critics of freer immigration. Surprisingly, their arguments are similar to ones used by progressives who argued for immigration restrictions in the early 20th century. Then, as now, those arguments fail to justify immigration restrictions.

A freer and deregulated immigration policy is fully consistent with the values held by American conservatives.

Two facts are required to understand the current state of America's immigration system. The first is that immigration is the voluntary movement of individuals to the United States. Immigration is not the government-funded or forced movement of people. Thus, if America's immigration laws were liberalized, the likely increase in lawful immigration would be the result of free individuals deciding to immigrate.

Second, current U.S. immigration policy is heavily restricted. Most available green cards are set aside for family members, with small numbers available to highly skilled workers, refugees, and beneficiaries of a government-run green-card lottery. There is currently no green card available for a low-skilled immigrant without an American family. The Ellis Island model of free immigration ended a long time ago.

The United States allows more legal immigrants every year than any other nation.

However, the percentage of immigrants each year *compared with* our population is small relative to most developed countries. Each year, immigrant inflows to the United States equal about 0.34 percent of our population. In comparison, countries like Canada, Australia, and Switzerland annually let in immigrants equal to 0.8 percent, 0.9 percent, and 1.8 percent of their respective populations. In other words, Switzerland's immigration policy is six times more open than the United States' immigration policy.

AMERICA'S TRADITIONAL IMMIGRATION POLICY

Traditionally, America's immigration policy was far more open than today's. The Declaration of Independence complained that King George III restricted migration to the colonies. Although Congress can control naturalization – the process of becoming an American citizen – there is no enumerated power in the Constitution that allows Congress to restrict

Government-created restrictions on the movement of peaceful and healthy people violate the natural right to free movement.

the movement of immigrants here. The Supreme Court later determined that Congress did have that power, in addition to many other powers not enumerated.

The Naturalization Act of 1790 set rules for naturalization but did not limit immigration. That federal policy of open borders reigned until the Civil War, when Congress actually subsidized immigration by exempting immigrants from the draft and allowing them to apply for cheap grants of western land under the Homestead Act.

In 1875, Congress passed the first federal restriction on immigration aimed at criminals and other "undesirables." In 1882, Congress passed the Chinese Exclusion Act to bar all Chinese immigrants. Between then and the 1920s, a coalition of labor unions, progressives, eugenicists, and nationalists successfully lobbied to restrict immigration. In 1921, Congress passed the first quotas on European immigration that emphasized family reunification – the grandfather of the current immigration system. Beginning in World War II, Congress began to gradually liberalize immigration. Presidents Ronald Reagan and George H. W. Bush were the last to sign major immigration liberalizations into law.

Since 1990, Congress has passed strict immigration-enforcement laws but has failed to further liberalize legal immigration. The result of our current immigration policy is 11 million to 12 million illegal immigrants living in the United States, enormous immigration backlogs, and no legal immigration option for most people who want to come.

* * *

America's founding ideologies of free-market capitalism, limited government, and individual liberty strongly support a freer immigration policy.

America's core founding principle is the Enlightenment theory of natural rights. According to that theory, each individual has inalienable rights to life, liberty, and private property that are not granted by any government. Freedom of movement is indispensable to the full use of those rights. To restrict an immigrant's ability to move to the United States not only infringes upon his natural rights but also upon the natural rights of Americans who want to hire that immigrant, sell him goods and services, and otherwise interact with him. Government-created restrictions on the movement of peaceful and healthy people thus presumptively violate the natural right to free movement.

Our English common-law heritage also has a strong presumption against restrictions on wealth-creating, mutually voluntary exchanges. Current immigration policies are just such a restriction. Under our common-law heritage, losses in income caused by economic competition do not justify compensation. Similarly, if an immigrant worker competes with a native-born American worker, the latter cannot sue the former for damages. Extending this logic to immigration biases our common-law heritage against restricting immigration.

Free markets require relatively minimal government control over the means of production: land, capital, entrepreneurship, and labor. Immigrants are both entrepreneurs and laborers, so their movement should be as legally unimpeded as possible to be consistent with the free-market standard. The phrase *laissez-faire* is used to describe the free-market system. Yet *laissez-faire* was once frequently paired with the phrase *laissez-passer* – "let them pass" – an admonition against government migration barriers within nations that distorted capitalism by impeding the movement of people toward economic opportunities. As laissez-faire also applied to international trade, so laissez-passer should also apply to international immigration. Laissez-passer is a neglected but vital component of free markets.

An ideology of free markets and individual liberty favors freer immigration. Since natural rights existed prior to government and do not derive from citizenship, the burden falls upon those who oppose freer immigration to show why it should be restricted, just as in other circumstances the government bears the burden to justify abridging citizens' rights to life, liberty, and private property. Such reasons could be based on legitimate national security, health, and criminal concerns, but they cannot be based on economic or cultural protectionism.

Current U.S. immigration law places the burden on the immigrant to prove to the government that he or she can immigrate – a situation analogous to assuming that all immigrants are guilty of an offense, and punishment will only cease once they prove their innocence. Such a lopsided immigration system is at odds with the intellectual underpinnings of the United States and should be repugnant to a free people. The justifications currently given for restricting the immigration of peaceful and healthy people do not meet the standards required to support such a severe government restriction.

ECONOMIC CASE FOR LIBERALIZED IMMIGRATION

Immigration increases the size of the economic pie by adding workers, entrepreneurs, and consumers to the U.S. economy, which then dynamically responds by accelerating the pace of investment and capital formation available for economic growth. Immigrants do not compete for a fixed supply of jobs but instead help improve the pace of employment and economic growth. In short, immigration boosts the supply side of the U.S. economy by increasing the number of workers and stimulating the growth of firms, while also stimulating the demand side by raising consumption of goods and services.

Immigrants' impact on the wage and employment prospects of Americans is the most contentious component of the debate over U.S. immigration policy. An increase in

Immigrants are both entrepreneurs and laborers, so their movement should be as legally unimpeded as possible to be consistent with the free-market standard.

the supply of labor through immigration would seem to lower all wages, but that conclusion is based on a static evaluation of a complex market. Holding everything else constant, an increase in immigrants would lower wages, but nothing is ever held constant in the macroeconomy.

Peer-reviewed research on immigration's dynamic impact on the labor market finds decidedly trivial effects. The most pessimistic findings are slight wage declines for a small percentage of workers, with many more American workers experiencing *increases* in wages *because of* immigration. There are many reasons that an increase in the number of people working and living in the United States would not lower the wages of most Americans and may actually raise them.

Not all labor is the same. For immigrant workers to lower the wages of U.S.-born Americans, both groups must have very similar skills and work in similar occupations. More immigrants increases the quantity of some *types* of labor, but the type of labor that immigrants perform is usually very different from the type of labor that U.S.-born Americans perform, meaning that there is little economic competition between most Americans and most immigrants.

Immigrants have very different levels of education than most Americans, so there is little direct competition between most Americans and most immigrants as well. Immigrants are overrepresented at the high and low ends of the educational spectrum. There are relatively few with the same education level of most Americans – limiting labor-market competition between Americans and immigrants. For instance, lower-skilled Mexican immigrants who work in landscaping are not going to lower the wages of American accountants, because the skills are so different that they do not compete.

Even when immigrants have similar education levels as those of American workers, there are still large differences in skill between the two groups. Lower-skilled immigrants typically have deficient English language skills. As a result of those differences in skills, lower-skilled Americans change their behavior in two important ways that shield them from competition with lower-skilled immigrants.

First, lower-skilled Americans react by

acquiring more skills through increased education to limit their labor-market competition with immigrants. Second, a division of labor occurs in which lower-skilled Americans specialize in jobs that require English communication. Those jobs tend to be higher-paying. Lower-skilled immigrants tend to specialize in jobs that require manual labor but not much spoken English, often pushing native-born Americans who are fluent in English up the occupation ladder. This has occurred in many sectors of the economy – including restaurants, where lower-skilled immigrants tend to work in occupations that emphasize manual labor, such as busboys, dishwashers, and janitors. Meanwhile, lower-skilled Americans tend to work in jobs that require English, such as waiters, hostesses, and managers. The latter occupations are all more highly compensated than those held by immigrants. This division of labor shields some lower-skilled U.S.-born workers from job competition with immigrants.

Immigrant and native skill levels are often

so different that labor-market complementarities emerge, which slightly raise the wages of U.S.-born workers. When American and immigrant workers are complementary, an increase in the number of one type of worker can increase labor-market demand for the other type of worker – raising wages in the process.

Immigrant workers also fill gaps in the U.S. labor market. Economist George Borjas wrote that mobility was the "core of modern labor economics." Immigrants are more mobile than American-born workers, willing to move long distances for job opportunities and away from areas in decline. During the Great Recession, lower-skilled Mexican immigrants were the most mobile workers in the economy and often moved great distances in search of low-paying jobs in other American states or even in Mexico. This movement lowered the supply of labor in distressed areas and increased it in growing areas so as to smooth the employment effects across the U.S. economy.

Increased mobility allows jobs to be filled more quickly, increasing the pace of economic growth. Internationally, immigrants primarily move to the United States when economic opportunities are expanding, and fewer come when there are fewer economic opportunities. The lack of welfare benefits for immigrants ensures that they move for opportunities, as they have very limited access to taxpayer funds in case of unemployment. This ebb and flow of workers across borders and within the United States produces a more stable economy that can react quicker to declines in growth and rebound faster during periods of expansion.

The demand for labor in the U.S. economy is also affected by immigration. Labor demand is primarily determined by the marginal value product (MVP) of the workers. This is the quantity of products produced by the workers multiplied by the market price for that product. For example, if a worker produces 10 widgets an hour that can each be sold for $1, then the MVP of the worker is equal to $10, and $10 is the maximum wage that worker could be paid.

An increase in widget-making laborers through immigration would increase the supply of widgets. As a result of the increase in the supply of widgets, their price will tend to fall. If the price of widgets falls slightly relative to the increase in the quantity of widgets, then the labor demand for workers and their wages will only fall slightly. If the price for widgets falls considerably relative to the increase in the quantity of widgets produced, then labor demand can fall and bring wages down with it. If the price of widgets remains the same due to elastic demand, then wages actually increase. Those results

---

An increase in the number of people working and living in the United States would not lower the wages of most Americans and may actually raise them.

---

affect varying sectors of the economy differently. The wage for agricultural workers falls far more than the wage for construction workers, for instance.

The MVP analysis reveals another effect of immigration restrictions. If the supply of workers in the United States falls because of immigration restrictions, the take-home pay for some workers would likely rise, but only because the price of the widgets they produce would also rise.

Agriculture provides an easily understandable example. Without a large supply of low-skilled immigrant farm workers, labor-intensive farming would either shrink dramatically or disappear entirely. American farmers would either grow fewer labor-intensive crops or stop farming. American consumers would either import fruits and vegetables from abroad or scale back their consumption of those foodstuffs – two options that are currently more expensive than employing immigrants in American agriculture. A shrinking agricultural sector or an increase in imports of food would be the economically efficient outcomes *if* increased labor scarcity were driven by changes in the free market. In the case of immigration restrictions, however, the increase in labor scarcity would be government-imposed and originate from legislation mandating more scarcity.

Immigrant entrepreneurship is another source of demand growth in the labor market. In 2013, immigrants were 72 percent more likely to start a business than native-born Americans, according to the Kauffman Foundation. As recently as 2011, immigrants were more than twice as likely to start a business as a native-born American. Entrepreneurship has two main effects on the labor market. First, it creates a job for the immigrant entrepreneur. Second, it has the potential to create a great many jobs for Americans at both the high-tech and low-tech ends of the economy.

Immigrants also counteract wage decline by increasing the demand for goods and services produced in the United States. Immigrants are consumers as well as workers. Many immigrants send percentages of their income abroad in the form of remittances, which partially returns to the United States in the form of increased American exports, but they also spend much of their money in the so-called nontradable sectors of the U.S. economy. The two most recent ethnic and racial groups that have immigrated to the United States in the past 50 years are Asian Americans and Hispanic Americans. Together they spend about $2 trillion annually. Services in the nontradable sectors of the U.S. economy, like haircuts and auto repairs, cannot be imported from abroad and are staffed by many low-skilled American workers. More immigrants consuming more products increase the labor demand for workers in those occupations, stimulating employment growth.

Immigrants also affect the capital market. Capital is an important component of economic, wage, and job growth. Worker productivity increases when the capital stock of machines, computers, and factories expands. Businesses increase the stock of capital in tandem with increases in the number of laborers. The relatively smooth adjustment of capital markets to immigration and population growth helps boost the productivity of workers and their wage growth, despite increases in the supply of workers.

Highly skilled immigrant workers in the science, technology, engineering, and mathematics (STEM) occupations increase the productivity and wages of all American workers. Economists Giovanni Peri, Chad Sparber, and Kevin Shih found that an increase of 1 percentage point in the immigrant STEM workers' share of total employment in an urban area raised the wages of American workers with a college degree by about 8 percentage points. American workers without a college degree saw their wages rise by about 4 percentage points because of STEM immigrants' effects on productivity. Growth in the immigrant STEM population likely explained a third to a half of the average productivity growth across U.S. cities from 1990 to 2010.

Immigration restrictions increase the scarcity of workers, which decreases the potential of the U.S. economy to grow and produce the goods and services we enjoy. Immigration restrictions are a pro-scarcity policy that results in a poorer economy even though the wages on paper, excluding the higher price those Americans would pay for goods and services, might rise for a few Americans. That the economy would adjust to artificially created labor scarcity does not justify establishing such scarcity through government immigration restrictions. The economy would adjust without immigrants, but the primary way it would adjust would be by shrinking.

Government Budgets and the Welfare State

If immigrant consumption of government services and welfare benefits is sufficiently greater than their tax contributions, the positive economic effects of freer immigration discussed above could be wiped out. Milton Friedman is commonly quoted as saying, "It's just obvious you can't have free immigration and a welfare state." Friedman also said that "there is no doubt that free and open immigration is the right policy in a libertarian state, but in a welfare state it is a different story.... The real hitch is in denying social benefits to the immigrants who are here." He continued by saying, "Look, for example, at the obvious, immediate, practical example of illegal Mexican immigration. Now, that Mexican immigration, over the border, is a good thing. It's a good thing for the illegal immigrants. It's a good thing for the United States. It's a good thing for the citizens of the country. But it's only good so long as it's illegal." According to Friedman, as long as the United States has a welfare state, then the proper immigration policy is one of salutary neglect and toleration of illegal immigration.

Much research on the fiscal and welfare effects of immigration has been conducted since Friedman talked about immigration and the welfare state. This research compares the costs of immigrant consumption of government programs with the tax revenue they generate and judges their long-term fiscal impact. If the taxes that immigrants pay and generate through growing the economy are greater than what they consume in government programs, then they are a net fiscal positive and not a cost to American taxpayers. According to the findings, immigrants either do not impose net fiscal costs on U.S. taxpayers

Immigrants mostly pay for their own consumption of government services or slightly decrease government deficits – especially in the longer run.

or they slightly decrease government budget deficits.

Immigrants mostly pay for their own consumption of government services or slightly decrease government deficits – especially in the longer run. Many of the largest government expenditures like education, welfare, and entitlements occur at specific periods of people's lives. The biggest government expenditure early in life is public education. An immigrant who arrives in the U.S. at the age of 19 does not receive public education that can cost the taxpayers upwards of $10,000 per year – an immediate savings.

The children of immigrants, especially if they are U.S.-born, will have access to public education, but the cost of educating the child must be compared with what their expected future tax payments would be. An English-fluent child of immigrants with a high school education will pay more in taxes than an uneducated child of immigrants. Just counting the cost of public education without the future tax revenue paid by the graduate would yield a consistently negative fiscal impact for *anyone*, because it would ignore the 40 to 50 years of employment and tax payments after graduation.

Means-tested welfare benefits are generally

unavailable to legal immigrants during their first five years of residency, are unavailable to illegal immigrants, and are denied to lawful migrant workers with the exception of emergency Medicaid. As a result, immigrants in poverty are much less likely to use welfare than similarly poor natives. Even when poor immigrants do use means-tested welfare, they consume a lower dollar amount than similarly poor natives. In an apples-to-apples comparison, noncitizen adults on Medicaid cost 42 percent less than native-born adults, while the cost of noncitizen children is 66 percent below the cost of benefits for citizen children of citizen parents. Immigrants tend to consume less private- and government-supplied health care than the U.S.-born.

Immigrants subsidize the entitlement programs of Social Security and Medicare. From 2002 to 2009, immigrants made 14.7 percent of contributions to Medicare Part A but only consumed 7.9 percent of all expenditures, contributing $13.8 billion more annually than they consumed in benefits. Natives consumed

$30.9 billion a year more than they contributed. Among Medicare enrollees, average expenditures were $1,465 lower for immigrants than for U.S.-born Americans. The differentials are largely the result of return migration, eligibility rules, and age differences between the typically older U.S.-born population and younger immigrants.

Social Security's finances are also improved by immigration. Stuart Anderson of the National Foundation for American Policy ran numerous immigration scenarios to test their impact on Social Security's actuarial debt. Anderson found that a moratorium on legal immigration beginning in 2005 would balloon the size of the actuarial debt by 31 percent over a 50-year period. However, an increase in legal immigration by 33 percent would reduce the actuarial debt by 10 percent over 50 years. Interestingly, the best fiscal results are when illegal immigration is tolerated, because illegal immigrants cannot receive benefits but pay Social Security taxes both directly and indirectly.

Immigrants will age just as everyone else does, so many of them will be net consumers of entitlements in the future. However, about 30 percent of immigrants return to their home countries before collecting Social Security and Medicare benefits. Such a high return rate contributes mightily to making long-run immigrant Social Security contributions a net positive under most estimates. Medicare and Social Security are fiscally unsustainable programs and need reform, but an increase in younger immigrants can delay that day of fiscal reckoning or provide a more positive cash flow to ease the transition to a more sustainable entitlement system or a reform of the current systems.

A short-term analysis of the fiscal impact of immigration in the United States by the Organisation for Economic Co-operation and Development found that immigrants paid more in taxes than they consumed – equal to about 0.03 percent of GDP from 2007 to 2009. Longer-term studies and projections that include the dynamic economic impacts of immigration and the resulting increase in tax revenue generally find a slight positive impact on long-run government finances. Interestingly, analyses that assume less immigration or the removal of illegal immigrants uniformly find that government deficits would increase as a result. The fiscal benefits and welfare costs of immigration are so small that they should not be the basis for supporting or opposing freer immigration.

Welfare does enormous harm to Americans and immigrants, despite the latter's low consumption. Further limiting noncitizen access to welfare would improve the fiscal and economic benefits of immigration. The 1996 Personal Responsibility and Work Opportunity Reconciliation Act (Welfare Reform) significantly reduced immigrant access to welfare benefits. An updated version of this law could restrict all noncitizens from receiving all means-tested welfare programs. Sophie Cole of the Cato Institute and I wrote a detailed analysis of how to actually restrict immigrant access to welfare. Building a wall around the welfare state is politically popular, feasible, and economically beneficial compared with building a wall around the country.

POLITICAL CONSEQUENCES AND ASSIMILATION

A prominent fear among conservatives and libertarians is that immigrants and their descendants will consistently vote for bigger government. If immigrants somehow shifted the institutions of the United States further away from free markets, then the long-term economic costs of immigration could, theoretically, outweigh the benefits. This fear should not be a concern, according to the most recent research into the political and institutional effects of immigration.

Comparing country scores and immigrant populations in the Economic Freedom of the World annual report reveals a positive correlation between stocks of immigrants and economic freedom – even over time. The more immigrants there are, the more economic freedom there is and will be going forward. The correlation is small, but it even holds at the national level of the United States – although slightly. The economic freedom scores for individual American states is slightly negatively correlated with stocks of immigrants over time, but that negative effect is more than made up for nationally, where economic freedom improved as a result of immigration.

Another complaint is that immigrants are poor and will vote for a larger welfare state. The American states each have very different numbers of immigrants, ethnic diversity caused by immigration, and control over the size and generosity of many welfare programs. Since 1970, no pattern can be seen between the size of benefits a family of three can receive under Temporary Assistance for Needy Families (TANF) and the level of immigration or increased ethnic and racial diversity caused by immigration. Controlling for other factors, in 2010 a California family of three could receive $694 a month in TANF benefits. But in Texas, an identical family could receive only $260. The size of the Hispanic population in each state is the same: 39 percent. For every California or New York with many immigrants, a diverse population, and a vast welfare state, there is a Florida or a

---

The more immigrants there are, the more economic freedom there is and will be going forward.

Texas with similar demographics but a smaller welfare state.

The size of welfare benefits and the degree of economic freedom in states like Texas cannot be explained by immigration or increases in ethnic diversity caused by it. Differences in economic and political institutions between states seem to be a far better explanation than demographic changes caused by immigration.

Forthcoming research from the Cato Institute on the expressed ideological opinions and political-party identification of immigrants, their children, and their grandchildren reveal rapid assimilation by the second generation and virtually complete assimilation by the third generation. The ideological and political opinions of immigrants and their descendants rapidly converge with those of Americans whose families have been here for four generations or longer.

Civic and cultural measures of assimilation for immigrants who decide to permanently stay in the United States is continuing at a pace similar to earlier waves of immigrants in the late 19th and early 20th centuries. English-language fluency is virtually universal by the second generation and complete by the third – a pace similar to that observed with previous waves of immigrants from Europe. University of Washington Professor Jacob Vigdor, the foremost authority on immigrant cultural and civic assimilation, writes:

While there are reasons to think of contemporary migration from Spanish-speaking nations as distinct from earlier waves of immigration, evidence does not support the notion that this wave of migration poses a true threat to the institutions that withstood those earlier waves. Basic indicators of assimilation, from naturalization to English ability, are if anything stronger now than they were a century ago.

Restrictionist concerns that current immigrants are not assimilating culturally, civically, or politically are unfounded.

NATIONAL SOVEREIGNTY AND THE RULE OF LAW

A common argument against returning to the freer immigration policy of our ancestors is that such a policy would diminish America's national sovereignty. By not exercising "control" over borders through actively blocking immigrants, as the argument goes, the United States government would surrender a supposedly vital component of its national sovereignty. But that argument is mistaken, as there is no inherent conflict between freer immigration and national sovereignty.

The standard Weberian definition of a government is an institution that has a monopoly or near monopoly on the legitimate use of violence within a certain geographical area. The way it achieves this monopoly is by keeping out other competing sovereigns, also known as states. Preventing invasion and stopping insurgents or potential insurgents from seizing power through violence is how the United States maintains its sovereignty, not through labor-market protectionism in the form of immigration laws. The main effect of our immigration laws is not to keep out foreign armies but to exclude foreign workers from selling their labor to willing American purchasers. As such, restrictive immigration policies have no impact on the integrity of America's sovereignty.

Relaxing or removing immigration laws would not infringe upon the government's national sovereignty any more than a policy of unilateral free trade would. If the United States would return to its 1790–1875 immigration policy, the U.S. military would still counter foreign militaries crossing U.S. borders or otherwise threatening the nation. Allowing the free flow of nonviolent and healthy foreign nationals does nothing to diminish the U.S. government's legitimate monopoly of force.

The exception to this is the movement of people into the United States who would seek to destroy U.S. national sovereignty, such as foreign military forces, insurgents, spies, terrorists, or the like. Blocking entry to the vast majority of those who seek to undermine U.S. sovereignty is actually made easier by freer immigration for two reasons.

First, the government could more easily identify and exclude them through limited and targeted border controls that are currently difficult, because most government efforts target economic immigrants rather than security concerns. Focusing our scarce law-enforcement resources on actual threats would make them more effective. Second, if peaceful and healthy people could lawfully migrate, then anybody attempting to enter unlawfully would raise red flags – allowing the government to focus its resources on people most likely to be security threats. Our current restrictionist immigration policy and border controls likely impede the government's power to exclude threats to its sovereignty.

Historically, freer immigration and U.S. national sovereignty have not been in conflict. From 1790 to 1875, the federal government placed virtually no restrictions on immigration. During that time, the United States fought the War of 1812, the Mexican-American War, and the most destructive war in in our nation's history – the Civil War. The U.S. government's

Blocking entry to the vast majority of those who seek to undermine U.S. sovereignty is actually made easier by freer immigration.

monopoly on the legitimate use of force during that time was certainly challenged from within and without, but the government maintained its national sovereignty even with nearly open borders. We do not have to choose between freer immigration and continued U.S. national sovereignty: we can have both, just as our ancestors did.

Many of those who complain that freer immigration would reduce U.S. national sovereignty are also concerned that immigration reform and the legalization of some illegal immigrants would erode the rule of law. The rule of law does not mean that the government cannot ever change a law, nor does it mean that a law must be perfectly enforced before it can be changed. Numerous laws, from alcohol prohibition to the 55 M.P.H. speed limit, were changed prior to perfect enforcement. In the case of prohibition, the difficulty of enforcement was frequently cited as a reason for repealing those laws and legalizing alcohol.

The rule of law means that lawmakers,

judges, and citizens are all subject to the same laws. Intertwined with this – and highlighted by political philosophers like F. A. Hayek – is that laws and enforcement should be predictable so people can plan their lives within a stable legal regime. Laws must be nonarbitrary, consistent with our traditions as a free society, and applied equally to be consistent with the rule of law.

Immigration laws abjectly fall far short of these standards. California Associate Justice Harry E. Hull Jr. wrote that immigration laws are "second only to the Internal Revenue Code in complexity." As a result, the immigration laws are complex and arbitrary, preventing predictable outcomes of their application. Immigration law is not applied equally, because it treats immigrants differently based on distinctions such as country of origin, skill level, and familial relations. Furthermore, the modern labyrinth of immigration laws and restrictions is a radical departure from the relatively freer system of America's past. On each measure of the rule of law, our immigration laws as they currently stand actually violate that principle far more than any liberalization and legalization could.

If freer immigration were the law of the land, the government would not be able to arbitrarily stop immigrants for virtually any reason, the power of American bureaucrats to

---

A freer immigration system would be consistent with our principles of limited government, free markets, and individual liberty.

---

capriciously exclude immigrants and punish American businesses who want to hire them would be diminished, the outcomes of attempting to immigrate would be *ex ante* more predictable for the immigrant, and the U.S. government's power in relation to immigration would be brought in line with our traditions.

CONCLUSION

Immigration restrictions should be based on protecting the life, liberty, and private property of Americans from those most likely to infringe upon them – criminals, terrorists, agents of foreign governments, and the seriously ill. A freer immigration system would not only be economically beneficial to the United States, but it would also be consistent with our principles of limited government, free markets, and individual liberty. Immigration restrictions are tools used by the federal government to socially engineer the population of the United States, cater to interest groups, and satisfy anti-immigrant biases. It is high time those tools be removed or dulled considerably.

Open Immigration: Nay

"Give me your tired, your poor, your huddled masses yearning to breathe free …"

For the past five decades, America's immigration policy has been based on poetry. It needs, instead, to be based on prose.

Immigration is a federal government program, like farm subsidies or the Small Business Administration. As such, it must adapt in response to changing circumstances. What worked in the past may not work today.

Prior to the immigration-law changes shaped by Senator Edward Kennedy in 1965, the United States had experienced high levels of immigration in one period of its history: from 1848 (the year of the Irish potato famine and the suppression of revolutions in various European countries) to 1924, when Congress restricted immigration. This is a long time, to be sure, marked by major developments in our history, but only about one lifetime – before and after which our history is marked by other equally momentous accomplishments.

So immigration has been – and will continue to be – an important part of America's story. We are, indeed, a nation of immigrants. But we are also a nation of pioneers, inventors, explorers, slaves, slaveholders, horse thieves, and teetotalers. No one facet of our national experience captures the totality of it, and no aspect of our past can dictate the shape of future policies.

Even John F. Kennedy, nominal author of *A Nation of Immigrants*, the book that helped his brother pass the 1965 Immigration Act, understood that policies have to change with the times:

> *We no longer need settlers for virgin lands, and our economy is expanding more slowly than in the 19th and early 20th centuries.... [My proposals] will have little effect on the number of immigrants admitted.... The clash of opinion arises not over the number of immigrants to be admitted but over the test for admissions.*

Unfortunately, the changes passed in JFK's name have roughly tripled the level of immigration, from about 300,000 a year during his administration to 1 million today. Thus, in the 21st century, we are running a 19th century level of immigration. The mismatch between our modern society and the horse-and-buggy-era policy of mass immigration is the subject of this Broadside.

* * *

Before exploring that mismatch, it's important to outline the goals we seek for our society that might be affected by immigration. While there are obviously sharp differences over means, the broad middle of American society agrees on goals that the government should help cultivate – or at least not undermine. Among them:

➢ Physical security of our persons and property

➢ A strong sense of shared national identity

- Opportunities for upward mobility, especially for the poor, the less-educated, and generally those at the margins of the society

- The availability of high-wage jobs in knowledge-intensive, capital-intensive industries

- A large middle class, with a smaller gap between rich and poor generally being desirable

- A functional, responsible, and affordable system of social provision for the poor

Mass immigration undermines all of these goals.

But why should this be so? A century ago we permitted mass immigration, and it seems to have worked out. Putting aside the fact that mass immigration in the past was much more disruptive than we now remember, times have changed. The changes that distinguish a modern, mature society are hard to miss, and all of them – good or bad – point to the same fundamental break with the past.

In short, it's not 1914 anymore. Some examples:

ECONOMY. A century ago, what economists call the primary sector of the economy (farming, fishing, hunting, herding, etc.) still employed more Americans than any other, as it had since the dawn of man. Today, only 2 percent of our workforce occupies itself in this way. Meanwhile, the tertiary sector (service industry) now employs 80 percent, and climbing, of working Americans.

EDUCATION. Along with the change in the economy, education has become more widespread. Nearly a quarter of American adults had less than five years of schooling in 1910; now fewer than 2 percent have that amount. And the share of college graduates increased tenfold, from 2.7 percent to 27 percent.

TECHNOLOGY. In 1915, the first transcontinental phone call from New York to San

Francisco cost about $487, in today's dollars, for three minutes; the same call in 2000 cost 36 cents; and today, via Skype, it is essentially free. In 1908, a Model T cost more than two years' worth of the typical worker's wages; a Ford Focus today (a much better car) costs about six months' work.

GOVERNMENT. Total government spending (federal, state, and local) per person in 1900 was about $500 in current dollars; today it is about $18,000. All levels of government combined took about 8 percent of GDP in 1900; today the government takes 36 percent of GDP.

These and other changes have brought both benefits and woe, but modernization itself is irreversible. Whatever steps we take to accentuate the positive aspects of modern life and ameliorate the negative, the basic features of modern society are not subject to fundamental change. The developments briefly outlined above are inherent characteristics of a mature society; we cannot say that mass immigration would be fine if only we got rid of (fill in the blank), when what we fill in the blank with is an inextricable part of how we live today.

Mass immigration, despite all its difficulties, suited us during our national adoles-

---

No one facet of our national experience captures the totality of it, and no aspect of our past can dictate the shape of future policies.

---

cence. But maturity has changed our national metabolism, and what was once beneficial is now harmful.

As St. Paul wrote to the church in Corinth, "When I was a child, I spake as a child, I understood as a child, I thought as a child: but when I became a man, I put away childish things." Mass immigration is one of those childish things that we as a nation must put away.

THE BROKEN MELTING POT

The most important long-term measure of success in immigration is assimilation. The U.S. model of immigration has been based on turning immigrants and their descendants fully into Americans. This is unlike the experience of other countries, such as Germany or the Persian Gulf sheikhdoms, and even our own historical lapses (the slave trade, the Know-Nothing movement, and the bracero program for Mexican guest workers), which all have one thing in common – the willingness to import foreign workers without admitting them to membership in the society.

This process of Americanizing immigrants was tumultuous and wrenching for everyone involved, but it was eventually very successful. This has been possible because American nationality is not based solely on blood relations, like a biological family, but is more like a family growing partly through adoption. Immigrants attach themselves to their new country and embrace the cultural and civic values of their native-born brethren as their own.

But this offer of complete adoption into the American nation was always based on the requirement that the immigrant "assimilates himself to us," as Theodore Roosevelt put it. Such assimilation is more than the surface changes that are easily observed. Future Supreme Court Justice Louis Brandeis put it well in a 1915 speech, when he said that an immigrant is not fully assimilated until he comes to "possess the national consciousness of an American."

This is what Hudson Institute scholar John Fonte calls patriotic assimilation – an identification with Americans as the immigrant's new countrymen, "converting," in a secular sense, from membership in one national community to membership in another.

Unfortunately, the conditions of modern society make such assimilation increasingly difficult. This is not because of any intrinsic differences between immigrants past and present: the simple fact that most immigrants now come from Latin America and Asia, rather than from Europe, is of less importance with regard to assimilation than some observers seem to think. Instead, it is *we* who have changed.

Our modern society differs from the past in two major ways that relate to assimilation – one practical, the other political.

The first difference is technology. Easy and cheap communications and transportation over very long distances make it easier for immigrants to maintain ties with the old country, making it less likely that such ties will atrophy over time and thus focus the attention and affections of the newcomer (and his children) on his new country. This can lead to what scholars call transnationalism – living in such a way as not to be rooted in one nation but rather living across two or more nations, with one's emotional attachments similarly divided.

The desire to retain ties with family and friends back home is perfectly natural. But it was exceedingly difficult to act on in years past. Princeton University sociologist Alejandro Portes summed up the situation: "Earlier in the twentieth century, the expense and difficulty of long-distance communication and travel simply made it impossible to lead a dual existence in two countries. Polish peasants couldn't just hop a plane – or make a phone call, for that matter – to check out how things were going at home over the weekend."

But now they can. As a *New York Times* article put it: "Armed with cut-rate phone cards and frequent-flier miles, with modems, fax machines and videocameras, immigrants can participate in the lives of their families back home – be they in Barbados or Tibet – with an immediacy unknown to any previous generation."

The second, and perhaps more important, difference relevant to assimilation is the political change from the past: elites in all modern societies, including ours, come to devalue their own nation and culture and thus recoil from the very idea of trying to assimilate newcomers. This loss of confidence expresses itself in an ideology of multiculturalism, which rejects Americanization and promotes a kind of tribalism, with ethnic-group membership defining one's relationship to other Americans.

A century ago, the robust promotion of Americanization was a hallmark of all institutions, public and private, that immigrants encountered. The elites who run those same institutions today – in government, business, education, religion, philanthropy, journalism, etc. – might be most accurately described as post-American. They're not necessarily anti-American, but they lack the visceral emotional attachment to the national community that is the mark of patriotism. Instead, they see themselves as "citizens of the world" and thus are unwilling to cultivate in immigrants the patriotism that they lack.

Note that this resistance to patriotic assimilation does not come from the immigrants. Today's newcomers are no less or more inter-

ested in Americanization than their prede-
cessors a century ago. Rather, it is America's
elites and institutions that are ambivalent – at
best – about assimilation. And this ambivalence
is not a superficial phenomenon that we can
change simply with the passage of a new law;
it is deeply rooted in every institution of our
society.

Because of multiculturalism, schools today
are utterly failing to pass on the history, heroes,
and legends of our past. In fact, schools are

---

*Mass immigration, despite all
its difficulties, suited us during
our national adolescence.
But maturity has changed our
national metabolism, and
what was once beneficial is
now harmful.*

---

more likely to engage in a deliberate policy of de-Americanization, having become a battleground in a "conflict between those who want to *transmit* the American regime and those who want to *transform* it," as John Fonte notes.

Research has actually documented our schools' de-Americanizing effect on children from immigrant families. Sociologists Alejandro Portes and Rubén Rumbaut studied thousands of children of immigrants in San Diego and South Florida over a period of several years. When first surveyed, a majority of students identified themselves as American in some form, either as simply American or as a hyphenated American (Cuban- or Filipino-American, for instance). After several years of American high school, barely one-third still identified as Americans, the majority choosing an identification with no American component at all, opting for either a foreign national-origin identity (Cuban, Filipino) or a pan-racial identity (Hispanic, Asian).

As the authors sum up, "The shift, therefore, has not been toward mainstream identities but toward a more militant reaffirmation of the immigrant identity for some groups (notably Mexicans and Filipinos in California and Haitians and Nicaraguans in Florida) and toward panethnic minority-group identities for others."

The combination of those two modern traits – transnationalism and multiculturalism – means that mass immigration today is much less likely to result in the kind of deep assimilation of the vast majority of immigrants and their children that is necessary for immigration to be successful. This is true regardless of the characteristics of the immigrants, because the problem is inherent to modern society and the way that modernity limits our ability to replicate the successes of the past.

Safety in Fewer Numbers

Modern America faces a unique security challenge. Advances in communications, transportation, and weapons technology make it relatively easy for enemies to get access to our home territory and stage deadly attacks. As the 9/11 Commission staff's report on immigration noted, "It is perhaps obvious to state that terrorists cannot plan and carry out attacks in the United States if they are unable to enter the country."

In a very real sense, the most dangerous weapons of our enemies are not inanimate objects at all but rather the attackers themselves. Thus keeping bad guys out – and keeping them off balance or apprehending them if they do get in – is a security imperative.

Given this modern security environment, mass immigration undermines our security in two ways. First, it overwhelms our administrative capacity to screen out enemies or locate and remove them if they're already here. And second, by creating large, constantly refreshed immigrant communities, it provides enemy operatives with cover. And like the other aspects of immigration, neither of these security concerns – workload or safe

> *Because of multiculturalism, schools today are failing to pass on the history, heroes, and legends of our past.*

haven – is a function of changes in the immigrants themselves from a century ago; instead, it is changes in our society that make these issues we cannot ignore.

The Homeland Security and State departments expend much effort in developing and improving the watch lists used to screen out terrorists and other malefactors. These efforts are inevitably backward-looking: they seek indications of evil intent in past actions and ties that we know about. Many killers are no doubt identified and excluded this way.

Unfortunately, very often there is no prior indication that a foreigner means to do us harm. But experience shows that conventional immigration enforcement – not specifically focused on security threats but on simple immigration violations – can exclude a large portion of potential terrorists in the U.S., whether we know their intentions ahead of time or not.

From the 9/11 hijackers, none of whom should have been issued visitor visas, given their lack of ties back home; to the Fort Dix plotters, who snuck across the border; to visa overstayer and illegal worker Amine el-Khalifi, who plotted to bomb the Capitol building in 2012, most terrorists seeking to strike the United States have been serial immigration violators and could have been stopped or kept out altogether simply through better enforcement.

But each layer of our immigration-control system – visa office abroad, the border itself, and interior enforcement – is faced with massive, unmanageable demand, which causes overwhelmed bureaucrats to wave people through without sufficient scrutiny. A century ago, how effectively aliens were screened may not have mattered much: the amount of damage a small, disconnected band of anarchists could do with some dynamite and a horse-drawn carriage was limited. But today's volume of immigration simply cannot be subjected to the level of labor-intensive scrutiny that's necessary in the modern security environment.

Whether considering State Department visa officers, Border Patrol agents and border inspectors, or immigration agents and adjudicators inside the country, the result is the same: fatalistic acceptance of massive lawbreaking by a demoralized bureaucracy.

The lack of sufficient scrutiny overseas, at the border, or inside the country is not something that can be remedied simply with better training or more technology, desirable as those might be. The real problem is systemic, the result of excessively high levels of immigration. The words of one government report on USCIS (which issues green cards and the like) apply to the entire system: "It would be impossible for USCIS to verify all of the key information or interview all individuals related to the millions of applications it adjudicates each year … without seriously compromising its service-related objectives."

But even if there were a magical way of resolving the problem of administrative overload, the second security vulnerability of mass immigration would remain – large, constantly refreshed communities of foreigners that provide cover and incubation for attackers. In today's world of cheap and easy communications and transportation, immigrant communities, however unwittingly, fit Mao's observation regarding China's war with Japan: "The people are like water and the army is like fish."

President George W. Bush used a different image in his address to the joint session of Congress after the 9/11 attacks: "Al-Qaeda is to terror what the Mafia is to crime." The comparison is instructive. During the great wave of immigration around the turn of the century, and for some time after immigration was stopped in the 1920s, law enforcement had very little luck in penetrating the Mafia.

This was because immigrants lived in enclaves with limited knowledge of English, were suspicious of government institutions, and clung to Old World prejudices and attitudes like omertà (the Sicilian code of silence).

But with the end of mass immigration, the assimilation of Italian immigrants and their children accelerated, and the offspring of the immigrants developed (as a result of inculcation) a sense of genuine membership and ownership in America – "patriotic assimilation." It was this process that drained the water within which the Mafia had been able to swim, allowing law enforcement to do its job more effectively and eventually cripple the Mafia.

In the same way, reductions in immigration will promote more rapid assimilation in immigrant communities and thus make it harder for terrorists and other malefactors to operate there – harder to find cover, harder to recruit sympathizers, harder to raise funds. This is as true for Muslim immigrant communities as for Central American ones, which serve as home and haven for hyperviolent transnational gangs.

There is no question that other security measures may also be needed, such as improved intelligence-gathering overseas or even military strikes. But without cuts in both permanent and temporary immigration, we are leaving ourselves open to the enemy.

CHEAP LABOR VS. MODERN AMERICA

The key to the economic aspect of the conflict between mass immigration and modern society is the fact that immigration floods the job market with low-skilled workers. This results in a buyer's market for labor, in which employers can pick and choose among workers rather than having to compete with one another to attract and keep staff.

This has two major implications for the economy. First, a loose labor market reduces the bargaining power of workers compared with that of employers, resulting in lower earnings and less opportunity for advancement for the poor – both immigrants and native-born. And second, by artificially keeping wages lower than they would be otherwise, mass immigration reduces the incentives for more-efficient use of labor, slowing the natural progress of mechanization in the low-wage industries where immigrants are concentrated.

Mass immigration today is much less likely to result in the kind of deep assimilation that is necessary for immigration to be successful.

In other words, while immigration certainly increases the overall size of our economy, it subverts the widely shared economic goals of a modern society: a large middle class open to all; working in high-wage, knowledge-intensive, and capital-intensive jobs that exhibit growing labor productivity; and avoiding too skewed a distribution of income.

Immigration has always added workers to the economy, of course, but today is different because our economy has changed dramatically since the end of the first great immigration wave. Earlier immigrants came to an America still settling the frontier and then undergoing the titanic process of industrialization. Today we are in a postindustrial era, with barely 20 percent of our workforce in farming or manufacturing.

Into this 21st century economy, we have resumed the importation of what amounts to 19th century foreign labor. The contrast with American workers is stark. Among people in the prime working ages, 25 to 65, only about 7 percent of the native-born have less than a high school education, compared with 28 percent of the foreign-born. And the flow has been large enough to skew the labor market: while immigrants account for about 16 percent of all workers, they make up fully 44 percent of workers lacking a high school degree, resulting in an artificially bloated low-skilled labor force.

The effect of the ongoing surge of immigration on the incomes of low-skilled Americans is a textbook case of supply and demand. In fact, in his famous textbook, economist Paul Samuelson wrote specifically about the pre-1965 low-immigration policies: "By keeping labor supply down, immigration policy tends to keep wages high."

A change in that policy has had the inevitable effect. The National Research Council estimated that immigration was responsible for nearly half the decline in wages of high school dropouts from 1980 to 1994. In fact, immigration's overall economic benefit to Americans comes specifically from lowering the wages of American workers who compete with immigrants. Harvard economist George Borjas has calculated that the $35 billion net benefit to the economy from immigration (amounting to just two-tenths of 1 percent of

GDP) is the result of reducing the wages of natives in competition with immigrants by an estimated $402 billion a year, while increasing profits or the incomes of users of immigrant labor by an estimated $437 billion. In other words, mass immigration is an income-redistribution program that takes from the poor and gives to the rich.

The loose labor market created by immigration doesn't just reduce the wages paid to low-skilled American workers, but it also makes it less likely that they will be hired in the first place and more likely that they will drop out of the job market altogether.

Conventional immigration enforcement can exclude a large portion of potential terrorists in the U.S., whether we know their intentions ahead of time or not.

The share of working-age natives holding a job has declined as mass immigration has continued, going from 74 percent in 2000 to 71 percent in 2007 to 66 percent in 2014. The number of native-born Americans working today is lower than in 2000, despite significant growth in the population. That means all net growth in employment since 2000 – 100 percent – has gone to immigrants, and the number of native-born Americans who have dropped out of the labor market altogether is at a record high.

Immigration expansionists claim this is unrelated to the mass arrival of newcomers, because immigrants don't compete with American workers; instead, they do "jobs Americans won't do." Natives, however, dominate virtually every occupation in which immigrants are heavily represented – janitors, grounds-maintenance workers, maids and housekeepers, construction laborers, etc. If 73 percent of janitors are native-born, as they are, it's simply false to say that it's a job Americans won't do.

The other people who are harmed by ongoing mass immigration are earlier immigrants. As management theorist Peter Drucker wrote, "Immigrants have a mismatch of skills: They are qualified for yesterday's jobs, which are the kinds of jobs that are going away." And yet the success of immigrants who are already here is very much in our interest.

Over the course of this new wave of immigration that started in the 1960s, the immigrant population has been steadily doing worse relative to native-born Americans. Although immigrants increase their earnings over time, the gap between their earnings and those of natives has been growing for decades. While immigrant men earned slightly more than their native-born counterparts in 1960, by 1998 they earned fully one-quarter less.

The government-engineered superabundance of cheap labor also harms the future competitiveness of industries where the immigrants are most heavily concentrated, by slowing the spread of labor-saving – and thus productivity-increasing – innovation.

Capital will be substituted for labor when the price of labor rises, something the federal government's mass-immigration program is specifically intended to prevent. By artificially holding down the natural process of wage growth in labor-intensive industries, mass immigration thus serves as a kind of subsidy for low-wage, low-productivity ways of doing business, retarding technological progress and productivity growth. In effect, mass illegal immigration is an unintentional, but very real, Luddite force in our economy.

Germany experienced the same thing when it imported large numbers of Turkish and Yugoslav workers in the 1950s and 1960s. As Philip L. Martin and Michael S. Teitelbaum, two of the foremost scholars of immigration, have written, "Economists began reporting that the program was slowing investments in automation and mechanization, so that 'Japan [was] getting robots while Germany [got] Turks.'"

Historian Otis Graham tied together the

impact of mass immigration on American competitiveness and on its workforce: "The U.S. can either evolve towards a high-technology economy with a labor force of constantly advancing productivity, wage levels, and skills, or it can drift towards a low technology, low-skill, and low-wage economy, marked by widespread job instability and growing income disparity. Immigration policy will be important to the outcome."

Mass Immigration vs. the Welfare State

The conflict between mass immigration and modern America is clearest when looking at government spending. The combined spending by federal, state, and local governments accounts for more than one-third of GDP, a share many times larger than during prior waves of immigration. This includes welfare spending, of course, but also schools, roads, criminal justice, and other tax-supported activities.

The problem this poses was summed up by Milton Friedman: "It's just obvious you can't have free immigration and a welfare state."

Importing millions of poor people with large families means that by definition, they will pay relatively little in taxes but make heavy use of government services. This is true not because of any moral defect in the immigrants or any meaningful differences between today's immigrants and those of the past. Instead, it is *we* who have changed: our modern society embraces a larger role for government, expecting it to underwrite a system of social provision for the poor, education for the young, support for the elderly, a large portion of the nation's medical care, and many other functions, all funded by taxpayers.

There is no way to avoid this conflict between mass immigration and modern government services – welfare and the rest are inherent to modern society. Efforts to trim government and reform welfare may well succeed to a degree. But whatever measures we might take in the future to limit its size and scope, Big Government is here to stay. As scholar Robert Rector has put it, "Transfer or redistribution policies are a pervasive, if not predominant, government activity in all modern societies." That means mass immigration, if allowed to continue, will remain a drain on public coffers – forever.

The fiscal threat that immigration now poses did not exist in earlier eras, when the government was much smaller. In 1901 the entire federal budget totaled $525 million, equivalent to about $14.6 billion in 2014 dollars. By 2014 the nation's population had quadrupled, but the federal budget reached $3.7 *trillion*, 250 times larger, in real terms, than in 1901.

This means that during the previous wave of mass immigration, the federal government spent less than $200 a year per American, in current dollars. Today it spends nearly $12,000 – a sixtyfold increase in the amount of government per person.

Households headed by someone without a high school degree (whether immigrant or native-born) receive much more in services

Without cuts in both permanent and temporary immigration, we are leaving ourselves open to the enemy.

from the government, of course. The Heritage Foundation calculates that on average in 2010, they received $46,582 in services, while paying $11,469 in taxes, resulting in a fiscal deficit of $35,113. Updated to 2014 dollars, that's more than $38,000, the price of a new Mercedes C300 sedan. So each time the federal government permits the settlement of an immigrant family headed by someone without a high school diploma, it is obligating the American taxpayer to give that family an annual gift of the equivalent of a Mercedes.

High rates of welfare use by immigrants are not merely a statistical assumption based on their low levels of education and consequent low earnings. Census Bureau data show that in 2010, the majority of households headed by immigrants from Mexico, Guatemala, the Dominican Republic, and Honduras used at least one means-tested welfare program, mainly Medicaid and food assistance.

Immigration expansionists who are unfamiliar with the realities of welfare reject such statistics as not credible because they suffer from the common misconception that welfare and work do not go together. And it's true that immigrants are slightly more likely to be in the labor market than natives. But welfare and work are not opposites – they're complements. In 2010, one-third of immigrant households with at least one worker were on welfare, and 82 percent of immigrant households collecting welfare included at least one worker. This is because our welfare system is designed to subsidize the working poor who have children, and that's a fair description of the typical immigrant. Immigrants aren't using welfare at such astronomical rates because they're lazy or seek to fleece Americans; rather, their low level of education means that in a modern economy, they can only command low wages, making them eligible for means-tested government benefits.

This dilemma cannot be resolved by walling off the immigrants from welfare by denying them access. This was one of the goals of the immigration and welfare-reform laws that were passed in 1996. Welfare reform in general appears to have worked to shrink some programs and encourage work. But the immigrant-specific provisions did nothing to reduce immigrant welfare use. First of all, there were numerous exceptions in the laws, and Congress almost immediately rolled back certain provisions. Also, many states (particularly those where immigrants are concentrated) took up the slack, resulting in nothing but a shifting of the processing of the welfare benefits from federal to state bureaucrats. Finally, the national-origin groups that were most likely to receive welfare before the law's passage saw the biggest increases in naturalization rates after its passage, because once an immigrant attains citizenship, the alien-specific welfare limits no longer apply.

The result of all this was that the experiment in excluding immigrants from the modern welfare system was a failure. After welfare use briefly fell in the late 1990s, it was back to the same levels within five years: in 1996, 22 percent of immigrant-headed households used at least one major welfare program, and in 2001 the figure was 23 percent. By 2010, it was 36 percent.

In a broader sense, it's simply out of the question for a modern society to do what it takes to prevent fiscal costs from immigration. Immigrants don't just cross a physical border when entering the United States; they also cross a "moral border," entering a nation that will not tolerate the kind of premodern squalor and inhumanity that is the norm in much of the rest of the world – and even in our own country during earlier periods of immigration. Are Americans prepared to allow people to die on hospital steps because they're foreigners? No. Are we going to deny immigrants access to the WIC program? Say the name of the program out loud and you'll get your answer: Americans are not going to deny *nutrition* to *Women, Infants, and Children.*

Walling immigrants off from government benefits once we've let them in is a fantasy. The 1996 welfare reform was a vast social experiment that taught us that fine-tuning welfare policy to limit the costs of immigration is doomed to fail. Reducing future immigration is the only way to solve this dilemma.

What Is to Be Done

So what should modern America's immigration policy look like? There are many facets to any such policy, including enforcement, temporary visas, and assimilation. But let us look specifically at the numbers: How many immigrants, and which immigrants, should the federal immigration program admit for settlement in the United States?

Since mass immigration is in conflict with the needs of a modern society, one might think the number should simply be zero. But instead of zero immigration, it's better to use the approach of zero-based budgeting: start at zero, since a modern society doesn't actually need any immigration, and then admit those specific categories of people whose admission is so compelling that it is worth risking the kinds of problems that this Broadside has outlined. Such an approach wouldn't start from the existing level of 1 million a year and attempt to work down. Instead, it starts from zero, then works up.

All net growth in employment since 2000 – 100 percent – has gone to immigrants.

Most immigration, regardless of the source or destination, has three components: family, employment, and humanitarian. Family-based immigration – admitting immigrants because they have relatives in the United States – is different from other categories because it involves a delegation of authority. The American people grant the right to their fellow citizens to decide, in their individual capacity and without any affirmative determination by the government, who will move to the United States.

Because the consequences of such individual immigration decisions are of great import to the society as a whole, their scope must be as narrow as possible, limited only to a foreign spouse or foreign adopted child.

This means eliminating altogether today's immigration categories for the adult siblings of citizens, the married and unmarried adult sons and daughters of citizens, the parents of adult citizens, and the adult sons and daughters of legal residents. These are grown people with their own lives, for whom "family reunification" is a misnomer.

Restricting family immigration to spouses and minor children of American citizens would still result in a substantial amount of immigration. The average number of such immigrants admitted annually from 2009 to 2013 was about 358,000, representing about half of today's family immigration. It is likely that once other categories of immigration were eliminated, this category would decline, since a large portion of U.S. citizens marrying foreigners are themselves earlier immigrants.

The next major component is skills-based immigration, which selects people based on education, skill, or experience, often with specific offers of employment. The five employment-based categories in current law are commonly imagined to provide for the immigration of the world's best and brightest – "Einstein" immigration, if you will. In fact, in addition to a handful of actual geniuses, the employment-based categories admit a wide array of ordinary people who should not receive special immigration rights. There's no reason any employer should be permitted to make an end run around our vast, mobile, continent-spanning labor force of more than 150 million people unless the prospective immigrant in question has unique, remarkable abilities and would make an enormous contribution to the productive capacity of the nation.

Perhaps the simplest way to approach this would be to admit anyone who scores above 140 on an IQ test. A more conventional approach would be to admit "aliens of extraordinary ability" and "outstanding professors and researchers," as defined by the top employment-based category in current law. In 2013, the number of people admitted annually under this targeted definition of skilled workers (including their immediate families) was about 17,000, and we could do without a cap as long as standards for admission are set sufficiently high.

The third major component is humanitarian immigration. Under this broad heading are three main parts: refugee resettlement (bringing refugees from overseas into the country), grants of asylum (reclassifying as a refugee someone who is already here illegally or on a temporary visa), and cancellation of

Walling immigrants off from government benefits once we've let them in is a fantasy.

removal (a grant of amnesty to an illegal alien whose deportation would cause "exceptional and extremely unusual hardship" to the alien's legally resident parent, spouse, or child).

The Refugee Act of 1980 foresaw an annual intake of 50,000 refugees and asylees per year. The average in recent years has been double that. We should set an overall ceiling for humanitarian immigration of 50,000 per year, with the element over which we have the most control – refugee resettlement – dependent on the numbers of asylum grants and cancellations of removal. In other words, an increase in asylum and/or cancellations of removal would trigger a reduction in available slots for refugee resettlement, and vice versa.

The result would be a legal immigration flow of about 400,000 per year, still higher than any other nation in the world but less than half today's level.

*   *   *

In an earlier era, mass immigration worked for America. Times have changed, but this outdated policy persists through sentimentalism and inertia. To overcome this, Lincoln's words should guide us: "As our case is new, so we must think anew, and act anew. We must disenthrall ourselves, and then we shall save our country."

First American edition published in 2014 by Encounter Books, an activity of Encounter for Culture and Education, Inc., a nonprofit, tax exempt corporation. Encounter Books website address: www.encounterbooks.com

Manufactured in the United States and printed on acid-free paper. The paper used in this publication meets the minimum requirements of ANSI/NISO z39.48–1992 (R 1997) (*Permanence of Paper*).

FIRST AMERICAN EDITION

LIBRARY OF CONGRESS CATALOGING-IN-PUBLICATION DATA

Nowrasteh, Alex.
Open immigration : yea & nay / by Alex Nowrasteh & Mark Krikorian.
pages cm. — (Encounter broadsides)
ISBN 978-1-59403-821-1 (pbk. : alk. paper) —
ISBN 978-1-59403-822-8 (ebook)
1. United States—Emigration and immigration—Government policy.
I. Krikorian, Mark. II. Title.
JV6465.N68 2014
325.73—dc23
2014040370

10 9 8 7 6 5 4 3 2 1